# THE POLISH ALPHABET

# the Polish Alphabet

*the symbols and sounds of Polish*

James Paul Wallis

GRIJBEN

The Polish Alphabet: The Symbols and Sounds of Polish
A Grijben book
ISBN 978-83-961739-4-2
Also available as an e-book

Foreign Language Study / Polish

First published 2022
First edition



Published by Grijben
Poland
www.grijben.com

# Acknowledgements

Special thanks go to Aleksandra Mihok, Kamila Król, Michał Gągała, Monika Mikicka and Anna Lesnau-Wallis for their indispensable help in the creation of this book.

# Introduction

Welcome to *the Polish Alphabet,* your guide to the Polish writing system and the sounds the symbols represent.

Discover the 32 Polish letters (including special characters such as **ą** and **ż**), letter combinations that make new sounds (such as **cz** and **si**), typical handwriting quirks, punctuation and how to type the special characters.

The sounds are explained in everyday language, with extra detail and mouth position diagrams for the trickier letters. In case, you're a fan of phonetic symbols, they're included too. And if you want to hear the sounds, you can listen to the recordings at *www.grijben.com/alphabet/pl.*

# How to use this book

The content of this book is set out in a deliberate order, starting from the basic letter sounds, progressing to letter combinations, then on to harder-to-pronounce sounds and other subtleties. So, for a comprehensive grounding, start at the beginning with *the Polish alphabet* on p.11 and work your way through to the end. Equally, the sections are self-contained, so you can dip in and out as you fancy instead, using the contents or index pages to find what you need.

And remember, as you go through each page, you can listen to recordings of all the sounds covered at *www.grijben.com/alphabet/pl.*

*Thanks for reading!*

*Let us know what you think: hello@grijben.com*

# Contents

# The Polish alphabet

Here are the 32 letters of the Polish alphabet, in alphabetical order:

a ą b c ć d e ę f g h i j k l ł
m n ń o ó p r s ś t u w y z ź ż

And just for good measure, here they are as capitals:

A Ą B C Ć D E Ę F G H I J K L Ł
M N Ń O Ó P R S Ś T U W Y Z Ź Ż

*For notes on handwritten letters, see p.38.*

### Vowels

Of the 32 letters, nine are considered vowels: a, ą, e, ę, i, o, ó, u and y. The remainder are consonants.

### Dictionary order

Each of the special characters ą, ć, ę, ł, ń, ó, ś, ź and ż is considered a separate letter in its own right. That affects the order of words in the dictionary. For example, dawny *former* comes before dąb *oak* because a comes before ą alphabetically. Another example is that words starting with ś come in their own section (after the section for words beginning with s).

### Foreign letters

Q, v and x are missing from the above list, as they're not part of the "official" Polish alphabet. However, Polish speakers do use these "foreign" letters for words and abbreviations taken from other languages, such as Xerox and DVD, and even in some Polish brand names, such as the television channel TVP or the radio station RMF Maxxx.

# Overview of the Polish writing system

## A phonetic language

In a phonetic language, to read a word aloud, you just sound out the letters one at a time from left to right. Polish is (mostly) a phonetic language. For example:

**Panama**
*Panama*

In Polish, each **a** in **Panama** sounds the same.

This means that (unlike English) once you know the rules about what sound each letters stands for, you can read out any Polish word, even one you've never seen before.

Most Polish letters (such as k) have similar sounds to their English counterparts. Some differ (for example, c is said like ts, so noc *night* sounds like *knots*). There's an overview in the *Basic letter sounds* section on p.18–19.

## Special Polish letters

ą ć ę ł ń ó ś ź ż

These letters are common in Polish. They may seem mysterious at first meeting, but you just need to learn the sounds they stand for. The easiest for the English speaker is probably ł, which sounds like an English *w*. So the familiar exclamation *wow!* would be written łał! For the others, check the overview in *Basic letter sounds* on p.14–15.

## Letter combinations

English has some standard letter combinations – for example, the letters *ch* typically combine to make a single sound, as in *chip*. Polish also has a number of combinations that you have to recognise. Here's an example:

**rzeka**
*river*

rz represents a single sound similar to the *s* in *measure*.

This and other letter combinations are covered on p.16–17.

## The subtleties of Polish sounds

You can get a long way with the basics and by using English near-equivalent sounds. However, you may want to improve your clarity to improve your chances of being understood, or simply to sound less foreign and more Polish. In which case it's worth looking at the Polish sounds in more depth. See *Advanced pronunciation* on p.19–26.

### Consonant clusters

Sometimes it's not the individual sounds that present a challenge, but the way they go together. Polish is full of consonant clusters that don't exist in English, or that appear in unfamiliar positions. Take this example:

**kto**

*who*

The combination **kt** at the beginning of a word may be unfamiliar, as no English words start with *kt*. However, you do get that combination within words, such as *des<u>kt</u>op*. So, arguably, your mouth can make the sound, but there is the mental challenge of putting it at the start of a word. One way to practise would be to repeat *des<u>kt</u>op*, but inserting a longer and longer pause between *des* and *ktop* each time

It can be a similar challenge with other unfamiliar clusters, such as the **ść** here:

**ość**

*fish bone*

**ś** is similar to the *sh* in *ship*,
**ć** is similar to the *ch* in *chip*.

Again, it may feel strange, as no English words end that way, but it's similar to the *shch* from when you say *po<u>sh ch</u>ips*. Try adding pauses to make it *"p-oshch-ips"*. Or go the other way: start with *"o-sh-ch"* and make the pauses shorter and shorter.

For all such clusters, it can help to take the sounds one by one and then practise running them together.

### Predictable stress

Last but not least, there is the question of stress. That's the part of a word that is highlighted by an increase in volume or a change in pitch. It's what makes the difference between ***<u>con</u>****tract* (a legal document) and *con****<u>tract</u>*** (get smaller). While the position of the stress varies in English, happily, it's entirely predictable for most Polish words – you simply stress the second-to-last (penultimate) syllable. For example:

| | |
|---|---|
| **<u>rze</u>ka** | **Pa<u>na</u>ma** |
| *river* | *Panama* |

There are some exceptions that are worth learning. See the section on *Stress*, p.27–29.

# Basic letter sounds

Compared to English, the Polish writing system is straightforward. Apart from some combinations and exceptions (covered later in this book), the letters generally stand for the same sounds wherever they are in a word (for example, in Polish, each **a** in **Panama** sounds the same). Here's an overview of the basic letter sounds.

| *letter* | *nearest English equivalent* | | *examples* |
|---|---|---|---|
| a | like the short *a* in *hat* | /a/ | **tak** *yes*, **Polska** *Poland* |
| ą | like the nasal *on* in *long* (*except when it isn't – see p.20*) | /ɔ̃/ | **są** *they are*, **ręką** *by hand* |
| b | like the *b* in *bats* | /b/ | **brat** *brother*, **torba** *bag* |
| c | like the *ts* in *bats* | /ts/ | **co** *what*, **noc** *night* |
| ć | one of two sounds almost like the *ch* in *chip* (*see p.22*) | /tɕ/ | **mieć** *to have*, **ćma** *moth* |
| d | similar to the *d* in *dog*, with the tip of your tongue touching the gums just behind the upper teeth | /d/ | **dom** *house*, **idę** *I go* |
| e | like the short *e* in *egg* | /ɛ/ | **efekt** *effect*, **ale** *but* |
| ę | roughly like the nasal *en* in *engrave* with an added hint of *w* (*or not – see p.21*) | /ɛ̃/ | **gęś** *goose*, **księżyc** *moon* |
| f | like the *f* in *fig* | /f/ | **fakt** *fact*, **ufać** *to trust* |
| g | like the *g* in *go* | /g/ | **gęś** *goose*, **długi** *long* |
| h | similar to the *h* in *huge* but even more raspy (*see p.19*) | /x/ | **hotel** *hotel*, **aha!** *oh!* |
| i | like the *ea* in *pea* | /i/ | **idę** I *go*, **lalki** *dolls* |
| j | like the *y* in *yell* | /j/ | **jajko** *egg*, **klej** glue |
| k | like the *k* in *skin** | /k/ | **koń** *horse*, **tak** *yes* |
| l | like the *l* in *lip* | /l/ | **las** *forest*, **klej** *glue* |

Feel free to ignore the phonetic symbols if they're not of interest.

*To be precise, k, p and t are "unaspirated" (*see p.25*).

| *letter* | *nearest English equivalent* | | *examples* |
|---|---|---|---|
| ł | like the *w* in *wet* or *few* | /w/ | łóżko *bed*, piłka *ball* |
| m | like the *m* in *mother* | /m/ | mam *I have*, tam *there* |
| n | like the *n* in *no* | /n/ | noc *night*, ten *this* |
| ń | like the soft *ny* in *canyon* | /ɲ/ | koń *horse*, słońce *sun* |
| o | like the short *o* in *hot* | /ɔ/ | oko *eye*, koło *wheel* |
| ó | both ó and u sound like the *oo* in *too* | /u/ | król *king*, ósmy *eighth* |
| p | like the *p* in *spin** | /p/ | park *park*, sklep *shop* |
| r | a rolled *r* (*see p.19*) | /r/ | radio *radio*, rower *bicycle* |
| s | like the *s* in *sit* | /s/ | stopa *foot*, pas *belt* |
| ś | one of two sounds almost like the *sh* in *sheep* (*see p.22*) | /ɕ/ | śnieg *snow*, roślina *plant* |
| t | similar to the *t* in *stun**, with the top of your tongue touching the gums just behind the upper teeth | /t/ | tak *yes*, pytać to *ask* |
| u | both u and ó sound like the *oo* in *pool* | /u/ | ulica *street*, kupić *to buy* |
| w | like the *v* in *very* | /v/ | woda *water*, trawa *grass* |
| y | halfway between the *i* in *bit* and the *u* in *but* | /ɨ/ | być *to be*, my *we* |
| z | like the *z* in *zone* | /z/ | zegar *clock*, prezent *present* |
| ź | one of two sounds almost like the *s* in *pleasure* (*see p.22*) | /ʑ/ | źle *badly*, bliźniak *twin* |
| ż | like ź –almost (*see p.22*) | /ʐ/ | żona *wife*, duży *big* |

Beware: these descriptions are based on so-called "standard English", so some may not work for you, depending on your accent.
*To check, listen to the sounds at www.grijben.com/alphabet/pl.*

# Letter combinations

## Special pairs

Most of the time, you can pronounce a word in Polish by just saying each letter one by one (much more than you can in English), but watch out for these pairs, where the letters combine to make new sounds.

| *letter* | *nearest English equivalent* | | *examples* |
|---|---|---|---|
| **ch** | identical to a raspy Polish **h** (*see p.19*) | /x/ | **chleb** *bread* |
| **ci** | like **ć**, one of two distinct sounds a bit like the *ch* in *chip* (*see p.22*)* | /tɕ/ | **ciasto** *cake* |
| **cz** | the other of two distinct sounds a bit like the *ch* in *chip* (*see p.22*) | /tʃ/ | **czarny** *black* |
| **dz** | like the *dz* in *red zone* | /dz/ | **dzwon** *bell* |
| **dź** | like the English *j* in *jam*, but with the tip of the tongue closer to the teeth, and the rest of the tongue in the Y position (*see p.22*) | /dʑ/ | **dźwięk** *sound* |
| **dzi** | like **dź** above* | /dʑ/ | **dziecko** *child* |
| **dż** | similar to **dź** above, but with the tongue in the R position (*see p.22*) | /dʐ/ | **dżem** *jam* |
| **drz** | like dż above | /dʐ/ | **drzewo** *tree* |
| **rz** | identical to **ż**, one two distinct sounds a bit like the *s* in *pleasure* (*see p.22*)† | /ʐ/ | **rzeka** *river* |
| **si** | like **ś**, one of two distinct sounds a bit like the *sh* in *ship* (*see p.22*)* | /ɕ/ | **siostra** *sister* |
| **sz** | the other of two distinct sounds a bit like the *sh* in *ship* (*see p.22*) | /ʂ/ | **szalik** *scarf* |
| **zi** | like ź, one of two distinct sounds a bit like the *s* in *pleasure* (*see p.22*)* | /ʑ/ | **zima** *winter* |

Technically speaking, "pairs" like this are called "digraphs" (**dzi** and **drz** are each three letters, so they're "trigraphs").

* *With* **ci**, **dzi**, **si** *and* **zi**, *the* **i** *can be sounded or silent (see p.23).*

† *In a few exceptions,* **r** *and* **z** *stay separate, as in* **zamarzać** *to freeze.*

## Consonants softened by i

In Polish, some so-called "hard" consonants (listed below) are said to become "softened" when followed by an **i** and then another vowel. There is no softening if the **i** is followed by a consonant or is at the end of a word. Here's an example of what happens to the letters **pi**:

| *position of* **pi** | *example* | *softened?* | *sound of* **pi** |
|---|---|---|---|
| followed by vowel | **piec** *oven* | yes | like *p y* in *gap year* |
| followed by consonant | **pić** *to drink* | no | like the *ea* in *pea* |
| end of a word | **głupi** *foolish* | | |

In **pić** (**i** followed by a consonant) and **głupi** (**i** at the end of the word) the **p** and **i** make their standard sounds as on p.14–15.

But in **piec** /pʲɛts/, the **i** is said to "soften" the **p**. Really, it's the **i** that changes from a full sound /i/ to be like a super-short **i** /ʲ/ or an English *y*, resulting here in a sound like the *p y* in *gap year*.

The following "hard" consonants can all be softened by **i** as above.

| *consonant* + **i** | *example of softening* | *phonetic pronunciation* |
|---|---|---|
| **bi** | **biały** *white* | /bʲawɨ/ |
| **di** | **dialog** *dialogue* | /dʲilɔg/ |
| **fi** | **fiolet** *purple* | /fʲɔlɛt/ |
| **gi** | **angielski** *English* | /angʲɛlski/ |
| **hi** | **hiena** *hyena* | /xʲɛna/ |
| **ki** | **kiedy** *when* | /kʲɛdɨ/ |
| **li** | **wanilia** *vanilla* | /vanilʲa/ |
| **mi** | **miód** *honey* | /mʲut/ |
| **ni** | **linia** *line* | /linʲa/ |
| **pi** | **piątek** *Friday* | /pʲɔ̃tɛk/ |
| **ri** | **gloria** *glory* | /glorʲa/ |
| **wi** | **wiem** *I know* | /vʲɛm/ |

NB The rules for the combinations **ci**, **si**, **zi** and **dzi** are very different (*see p.22*).

## Pronouncing double consonants

You can pronounce a double consonant (such as in **inny** *different*) in one of two ways.

### Option 1: separate sounds

The first option is to sound out each letter separately, the first being said quickly and unstressed. So **pana** (genitive case of **pan** *sir*) is said *"pa-na"*, but **panna** (*girl, unmarried woman*) is more like *"pan-na"*.

| *example word* | *approximate pronunciation* | *meaning* |
|---|---|---|
| **oddawać** | *od-da-vatch* | *to give back* |
| **lekko** | *le-k-ko* | *lightly* |
| **willa** | *vee-l-la* | *villa* |
| **inny** | *ee-n-ny* | *different* |
| **fontanna** | *fon-ta-n-na* | *fountain* |

### Option 2: single, extended sound

Instead of sounding each letter separately, some Polish speakers make a single, but extended, letter sound, especially in casual conversation. To make this doubled sound, you hold your mouth in position to make the letter sound slightly (but noticeably) longer than usual.

One way to understand this is to think of English phrases that have a similar careful pronunciation. A couple of examples would be *ten ale's* (short *n*) vs *ten nails* (longer *n*) and *book ace* (short *k*) vs *book case* (longer *kc*). Say them out loud and see if you can hear how the length of the *n* or *k* sound changes. Try to notice what you're doing differently in each pair in terms of how your lips/tongue/teeth move and how you breathe to make the sounds.

### Choose 1 or 2, but make it different

*Option 1* is perhaps more formal and deliberate, but whichever option you choose, it's worth making the effort with your pronunciation to distinguish these double letters from single letters. This is especially true where the use of a single or double letter results in a completely different word, as with **pana** and **panna** above. Other examples include **rany** *wounds* and **ranny** *wounded* or **leki** *medicine* and **lekki** *light*.

# Advanced pronunciation

## ch/h in depth

Both ch and h represent the same sound. It's made with your tongue near (but not touching) the roof of your mouth, towards the back. The closest English sound is probably the *h* in *huge* or *hew*. But for Polish, your tongue is further back to make it more raspy.

*Phonetics fans: it's /x/, a "voiceless velar fricative".*

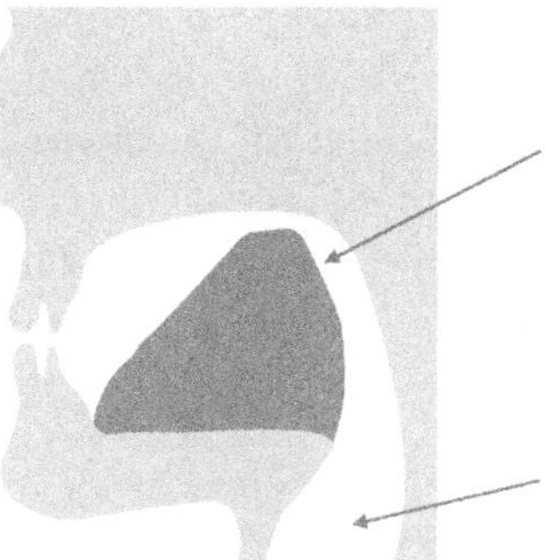


Make sure the sound comes from above your tongue and not from your throat.

## The rolled r

In Polish, the r is always "rolled". It's one of the harder letters for learners who aren't used to it, so if you get close, well done. You should at least try – it's absolutely not like the soft *r* you find in English.

You make a Polish r with the tip of your tongue (relaxed, not stiff) close to (almost touching) the gums behind your upper teeth, with air flowing past (breathe out) to make your tongue vibrate.

*Phonetics fans: this one is /r/, an "alveolar trill".*

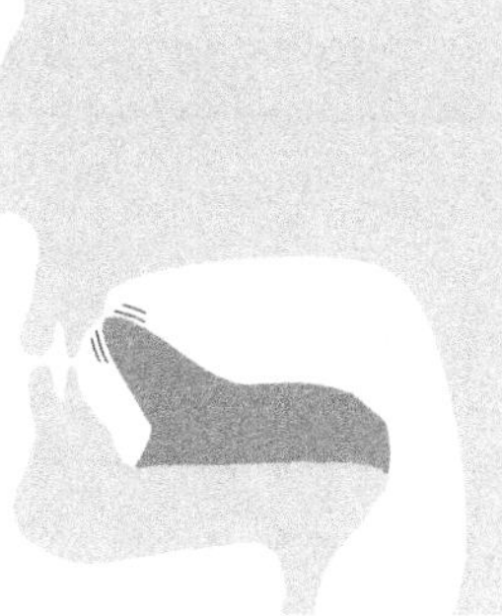

*The rolled* r *can be hard to pick up, but it is possible. If you're struggling, try a video tutorial – go to www.grijben.com/alphabet/pl. Keep at it.*

## ą in depth

"Officially", as it were, ą is a nasal sound /ɔ̃/ with no direct equivalent in English. It is similar(ish) to the *on* in *long* (the part of the sound before you get to the *g*, if you can imagine that), made with the tongue and lips not fully closed.

However, colloquially, when ą is followed by certain letters (see below), Polish speakers tend to pronounce it more like *on* (as in *gone*), *om* (as in *Tom*) or *ong* (as in *long*, up to and including the *g* this time). They're not trying to make your life harder of course – the changes come naturally from the effect of the mouth trying to jump smoothly from one sound to another.

If in doubt, you can always use the full "official" nasal sound – but if you pick up the changes, you'll sound more Polish. Enjoy.

| *position of* ą | *sound of* ą | *examples* |
|---|---|---|
| at the end of a word | keeps the full "official" nasal sound /ɔ̃/ | są *they are*<br>ręką *by hand* |
| before ch, f, h, s, ś, sz, w, z, ź or ż | again, keeps the "official" nasal sound /ɔ̃/ | wąski *narrow*<br>mąż *husband* |
| before c, cz, d, dz, dż, drz or t | sounds like the *on* in *gone* /ɔn/ | mądry *clever*<br>trójkąt *triangle* |
| before g or k | sounds more like the *ong* in *long* /ɔŋ/ | pociąg *train*<br>mąka *flour* |
| before b or p | sounds like the *om* in *Tom* /ɔm/ | gołąb *pigeon*<br>kąpiel *bath* |
| before l or ł | sounds like the *o* in *Tom* /o/ | wziął *he took* |

## ę in depth

The "official" nasal **ę** sound /ɛ̃/ has no direct equivalent in English. It's similar to *en* in *engrave*, but with a hint of a *w* (think *"ewngrave"*). You make the sound with the tongue and lips not fully closed.

As with **ą** (*see p.20*), the sound of **ę** in modern spoken Polish often varies though, depending on whether it's at the end of a word, or is followed by certain letters.

| *position of* **ę** | *sound of* **ę** | *examples* |
|---|---|---|
| before **l** or **ł**, or at the end of a word | tends to be said as a simple **e**, like the *e* in *hem* | **idę** *I go*<br>**wzięła** *she took* |
| before **b** or **p** | more like the *em* in *hem* | **zęby** *teeth*<br>**dostępne** *available* |
| in other positions (and especially before **c**, **cz**, **d**, **dz**, **dż**, **drz** or **t**) | tends to be said like the *en* in *ten* | **ręką** *by hand*<br>**pędzel** *brush*<br>**piętro** *storey* |

### Full pronunciation for clarity

So, hang on, when *do* you use the full, official nasal pronunciation of **ę**? You tend to hear the full **ę** sound only at the end of a word, where many native speakers use it interchangeably with an **e** sound (*see the table above*). You also use it if you want to pronounce something deliberately to be extra clear – for example, to show you mean **chcę** *I want* and not **chce** *he/she/it wants*.

*Listen to the sounds at www.grijben.com/alphabet/pl.*

## The difference between ś and sz

Polish has some pairs of sounds that may be hard for the learner to distinguish, but are distinct to the Polish ear and can affect meaning. Let's start with the example of the "rushing air" sound pair **ś** and **sz**.

They say that **ś** /ɕ/ is more like the *sh* in *sheep*, while **sz** /ʂ/ is more like the *sh* in *shark*. Be honest though, have you ever noticed that *sheep* and *shark* have different *sh* sounds? Probably not. Even if you do say them differently, it's probably not deliberate, and it doesn't really matter either, because no English words differ only in those sounds. With Polish, though, the difference in *sh* sounds (**ś** and **sz**) is deliberate and does matter. See for example **wieś** *village* and **wiesz** *you know*. The difference comes from whether your tongue is in the "Y position" or the "R position".

### The Y position (ś)

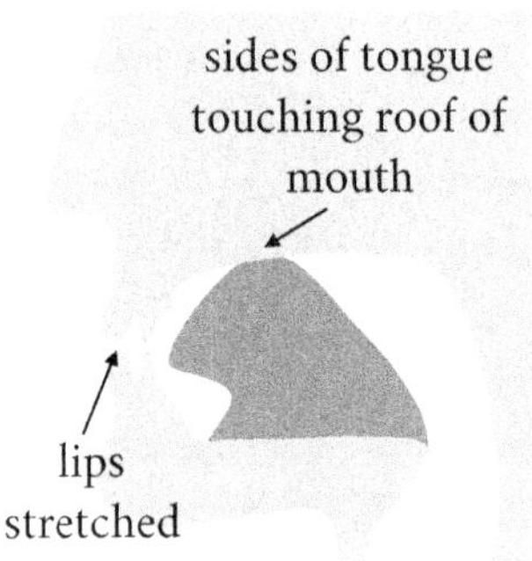


Imagine you are about to make an English *y* sound (as in *yes*), with the middle of your tongue curved at the sides to touch the roof of your mouth* – hold it in that position and breathe out. You stretch your lips slightly as you do it, as though smiling.
This is a "palatal fricative".

### The R position (sz)

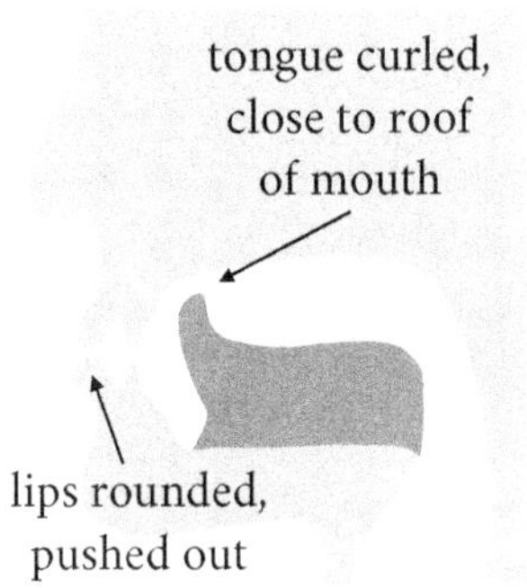


Imagine you are about to make an English *r* sound (as in *red*), with the end of your tongue curled up slightly towards the roof of your mouth* – now hold it in that position and breathe out. You purse your lips slightly as you do it.
This is a "retroflex fricative".

Note that done properly, **ś** is a higher-pitched rushing sound than **sz**.

**For the start of ć/ci or dź/dzi, the tip of your tongue touches the upper gum ridge briefly too.*

## The other pairs like ś and sz

So, OK, Polish has a pair of two different *sh* sounds, ś and sz. Similarly, there are two sounds like the *ch* in *cheese*, two like the *s* in *treasure*, and two like the *j* in *jam*. Here they are, in that order, in a table. In each pair, the rushing air part comes from the Y or R position.

What about ci, si, zi and dzi? Well, they have the same initial sound as ć, ś, ź and dź, and the i is sounded or silent (see next section). Meanwhile, ż and rz are identical, as are dż and drz.

| *Y position* | | *examples* | *R position* | | *examples* |
|---|---|---|---|---|---|
| ć | /tɕ/ | mieć *to have* | cz | /tʂ/ | miecz *sword* |
| ci | | ciasto *cake* | | | |
| ś | /ɕ/ | śnieg *snow* | sz | /ʂ/ | masz *you have* |
| si | | siedem *seven* | | | |
| ź | /ʑ/ | źle *bad* | ż | /ʐ/ | żona *wife* |
| zi | | zima *winter* | rz | | rzeka *river* |
| dź | /dʑ/ | dźwięk *noise* | dż | /dʐ/ | dżem *jam* |
| dzi | | dziura *hole* | drz | | drzewo *tree* |

### The i in ci, dzi, si and zi – sounded or silent?

You'll see in the table above that there are two ways to write each Y-position sound. Take si as an example. The initial sound is identical to ś (*see above and p.22*), while the i is either sounded or silent as follows.

- **Silent i**: when si is followed by a vowel (e.g. siano *hay*), it just stands for a ś sound. No actual i sound occurs.
- **Sounded i**: when si is at the end of the word (e.g. musi *he/she/it must*) or followed by a consonant (e.g. silny *strong*), the i is sounded (like the *ea* in *pea*).

The same rules apply for the i in ci, zi, and dzi. So ciasto *cake* is said like *cha-sto* (not *chee-a-sto*), but cicho *quietly* is said like *chee-ho*.

*Listen to the sounds at www.grijben.com/alphabet/pl.*

## Devoicing of consonants

A pronunciation quirk to be aware of in Polish is the so-called "devoicing" of consonants. The voiced consonants (see table below) get "devoiced" when they (a) land at the end of a word (so **ząb** is said "**ząp**") or (b) are next to (either before or after) an unvoiced consonant (so **kwiat** is said "**kfiat**"). Here are some examples:

| *voiced* | | *devoiced* | *example of devoicing* |
|---|---|---|---|
| b | → | p | ząb ("ząp") *tooth* |
| d | → | t | lód ("lót") *ice* |
| dz | → | c | szwedzki ("szwecki") *Swedish* |
| dź | → | ć | idź ("ić") *go! (you, informal)* |
| dż | → | cz | brydż ("brycz") *bridge (card game)* |
| g | → | k | pociąg ("pociąk") *train* |
| rz | → | sz | trzy ("tszy") *three* |
| w | → | f | kwiat ("kfiat") *flower* |
| z | → | s | bluzka ("bluska") *blouse* |
| ź | → | ś | znaleźć ("znaleść") *to find* |
| ż | → | sz | łóżko ("łószko") *bed* |

Now, you could argue that this is fairly advanced stuff, in that Polish speakers will fully understand you, even if you don't devoice these consonants. However, it is an extremely common phenomenon, and occurs with many basic words like **też** (said like "**tesz**"). You should at least be aware of devoicing for when you're listening to other people.

**Voiced vs unvoiced**

To be clear on what we're talking about here, consider the English letters *f* and *v*. They're both made with air flowing through the lips and teeth in the same way, but *f* is "unvoiced" (there is no accompanying noise made by the vocal cords) while *v* is "voiced" (there is an accompanying vibrating noise). Try saying *alive* and *a life* to hear the difference.

## Unaspirated k, p, t

In Polish, all consonants are pronounced "unaspirated". That's different from English, where *k*, *p* and *t* in particular are aspirated in many words – that is, they're said with a small puff of air. The trick for aspiring (pun intended) speakers of Polish is to learn to say **k**, **p** and **t** without the puffs.

> *Admittedly, this "aspirated" vs. "unaspirated" business is pretty subtle. You'll be understood well enough even if you aspirate some Polish letters where a native speaker wouldn't. But if you can pick this up, it's another step towards sounding more Polish. It all helps.*

### No puff of air

Many native English speakers use both aspirated and unaspirated consonant sounds without even thinking about it. As an example, the *p* is typically aspirated in *pin*, but unaspirated in *spin*. Try saying them slowly to see if you can hear/feel the difference. (It might help to whisper them to make the difference clearer. Or try holding a piece of paper in front of your mouth and then watch whether it moves as you say each word.)

Now, in Polish, the **p** is always unaspirated. To practise that, see if you can say *pin* in English but with an unaspirated *p* – start by saying *spin*, then leave a slight pause between the *s* and the *pin* (without changing the *p* sound!), and then drop the *s* altogether. If you can do that, you've got it.

For more practice, try saying these word pairs – aspirated English first, unaspirated Polish second. Check that you notice a difference.

| | | |
|---|---|---|
| *carp* **karp** | *paper* **papier** | *tennis* **tenis** |
| *Krakow* **Kraków** | *perfume* **perfumy** | *tourist* **turysta** |
| *cousin* **kuzyn** | *Poland* **Polska** | *type* **typ** |

*Listen to the sounds at www.grijben.com/alphabet/pl.*

## Vowel groups

Many words in Polish have groups of two vowels. In theory, each vowel is pronounced separately, but there are common exceptions.

### Separated vowel sounds

In the following examples, Polish speakers keep the vowels separate (you might even hear the slight pause between vowels that keeps them apart), making **teatr** sound like **te-atr**, with no extra sounds.

| zainstalować | teatr | choinka |
|---|---|---|
| *to install* | *theatre* | *spruce/Christmas tree* |

That's different from English, where you can add mini-sounds to smooth things out and slide from one vowel to the next (for example, *theatre* is said like *"the-ya-ter"*). In Polish, keep them separate.

### Exceptions – au and eu

The combination **au** is said as though it were written **ał** to sound like the *ow* in *cow*. You hear this in words such as these on the right. (But not in words like **nauczyć** *teacher*, which is formed from **na** + **uczyć**.)

**restauracja**
*restaurant*
**autobus**
*bus*

**muzeum** *museum*
**Europa** *Europe*
**eukaliptus** *eucalyptus*

Similarly, **eu** is said as though it were written **eł** to sound like the *airw* in *hair wax*. You hear this in words such as those on the left.

### More exceptions – i + vowel

Polish is full of words that include an **i** followed by another vowel (maybe even a second **i**). In most of these, though, the **i** isn't really an **i** – it has combined with a preceding consonant and become more like the *y* in *yes* (*see p.17*). Here, you do get that sliding effect mentioned above. For example, you get the same slide from **n** to **o** in the Polish **kanion** and English *canyon*. More examples:

| miasto | nie | wiosna | biuro | w linii |
|---|---|---|---|---|
| *town/city* | *no* | *spring* | *office* | *in a line* |

Even more extreme is where the **i** has combined with a preceding **c**, **s** or **z** but is itself silent (*see p.23*). For example:

| ciasto | siedem | zielony | dziura |
|---|---|---|---|
| *cake* | *seven* | *green* | *hole* |

# Stress

## Standard stress: second-to-last syllable

By and large, the stress falls on the second-to-last (penultimate) syllable of Polish words (so if there are only two syllables, the first one is stressed). For example (stressed syllable underlined in **bold**):

| | | |
|---|---|---|
| **sie**dem *seven* | her**ba**ta *tea* | czer**wo**ny *red* |
| **te**raz *now* | sa**mo**chód *car* | fiole**to**wy *purple* |

This means that the stress can move around when a word is altered in a way that changes the number of syllables, such as with a change of case, conjugation of a verb, or even just being made plural. Look at these examples:

| | | | |
|---|---|---|---|
| singular vs plural noun → | jeden **ro**wer<br>*one bicycle* | *BUT* | dwa ro**we**ry<br>*two bicycles* |
| change of case (acc. vs instr.) → | mam sa**mo**chód<br>*I have a car* | *BUT* | jadę samo**cho**dem<br>*I go by car* |
| singular vs plural verb → | **mó**wię cicho<br>*I speak quietly* | *BUT* | mó**wi**my cicho<br>*we speak quietly* |

### A note on syllable counting and i

When you're working out which is the second-to-last syllable, bear in mind that in many words, the i is not fully pronounced (*see p.17*) and so doesn't count as a separate syllable. Typically, ia, ie, ii, io and iu are said as single syllables (sounding like *ya, yeah, yee, yo, you*).

Some examples:

The name **A**nia has two syllables (A-nia) not three (it isn't An-i-a). **Sia**dać *to sit* has two syllables (sia-dać). The last syllable in biżu**te**ria is ria, so the stress is on the te. And here's the stress in **kos**tium kąpie**lo**wy *swimming costume*.

## Exceptions: third-to-last syllable

In some words, the stress is on the third-to-last (antepenultimate) syllable (not the usual second-to-last as described on p.27). Here are the five main categories with some examples:

### 1 Numbers: 400, 700, 800, 900

The "hundreds" keep the stress on the syllable of the original number before **sta** or **set** was tagged on. That means 400, 700, 800 and 900 don't follow the last-but-one rule.

| | | | | | |
|---|---|---|---|---|---|
| 100 | **sto** | 400 | **czterysta** | 700 | **siedemset** |
| 200 | **dwieście** | 500 | **pięćset** | 800 | **osiemset** |
| 300 | **trzysta** | 600 | **sześćset** | 900 | **dziewięćset** |

### 2 Words of foreign origin

Some words taken from foreign languages (particularly Latin and Greek) have the stress on the third-but-one syllable.

There are some examples to learn, but the best practice is just to notice the unusual stress when you first hear a word – or at least be aware that some words are unusual, so you don't drop your **pieróg** with surprise when you spot one.

**botanika** *botany*
**ceramika** *ceramics*
**fizyka** *physics*
**klinika** *clinic*
**informatyka** *IT*
**matematyka** *mathematics*
**muzyka** *music*
**prezydent** *president*
**technika** *technology*
**turystyka** *tourism*
**uniwersytet** *university*

Other examples include **Ameryka** *America* and **Korsyka** *Corsica.*

### 3 Acronyms

Where you say the acronym by spelling out each letter, the final letter is stressed. Such as: **TVP** (a TV broadcaster), **PKP** (the national railway service), **RMF FM** (a radio station).

However, acronyms that can be spoken as though they were words follow the usual last-but-one-syllable stress rule. For example:

**NATO** (*the North Atlantic Treaty Organisation)*
**OBOP** (*a public opinion research centre)*

### 4 Past tense: first/second person plural

To start, a confession: outside of official or formal contexts, many modern Polish speakers ignore the exception described below and pronounce all past tense forms with the stress on the penultimate syllable, as per the standard rule. Arguably, you could ignore it too, and still sleep soundly.

The traditional, formal rule, though, is that for the first and second person plural forms in the past tense (which have longer endings than the others), the stress falls on the third-to-last syllable.

Here's how the formal rule looks with **lubić** *to like* as an example:

| | |
|---|---|
| lu<u>bi</u>łem, lu<u>bi</u>łam | *I liked* |
| lu<u>bi</u>łeś, lu<u>bi</u>łaś | *you (singular) liked* |
| <u>lu</u>bił, lu<u>bi</u>ła, lu<u>bi</u>ło | *he/she/it liked* |
| lu<u>bi</u>liśmy, lu<u>bi</u>łyśmy | *we liked* |
| lu<u>bi</u>liście, lu<u>bi</u>łyście | *you (plural) liked* |
| lu<u>bi</u>li, lu<u>bi</u>ły | *they liked* |

### 5 Conditional forms

Here, we're talking about conditional forms such as **lubiłaby** *she would like*. (Note: like the exception about the past tense above, the following is not followed by all Polish speakers all of the time.)

You can think of the conditional forms as being made by taking a stem (namely the past tense third person singular forms) and tagging on conditional endings (**-bym**, **-byś**, **-by**, **-byśmy**, **-byście** or **-by**).

The stress-rule exception here is that although you count the syllables to find the last-but-one syllable to stress as normal, you ignore the endings.

Here's the conditional tense of **lubić** *to like* as an example:

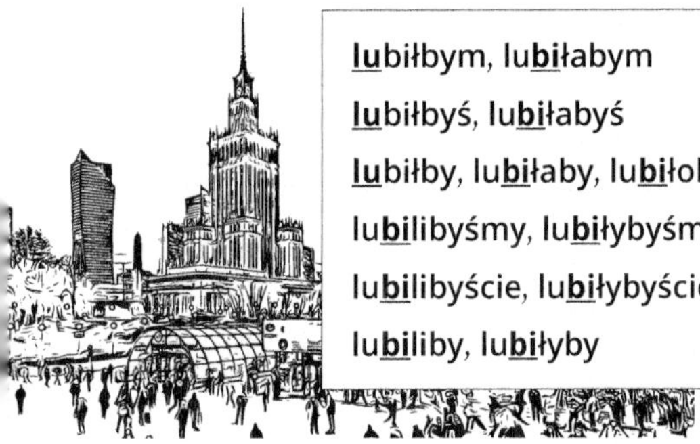

| | |
|---|---|
| <u>lu</u>biłbym, lu<u>bi</u>łabym | *I would like* |
| <u>lu</u>biłbyś, lu<u>bi</u>łabyś | *you (singular) would like* |
| <u>lu</u>biłby, lu<u>bi</u>łaby, lu<u>bi</u>łoby | *he/she/it would like* |
| lu<u>bi</u>libyśmy, lu<u>bi</u>łybyśmy | *we would like* |
| lu<u>bi</u>libyście, lu<u>bi</u>łybyście | *you (plural) would like* |
| lu<u>bi</u>liby, lu<u>bi</u>łyby | *they would like* |

# Spelling it out (aka letter names)

There are times when you'll want to ask how something is spelled, or tell someone how you spell your name etc.

## The easier ones

Let's tackle the more straightforward letters first.
(*Without wanting to spoil the surprise, the harder batch are on p.32.*)

| *letter* | *formal "letter name"* | |
|---|---|---|
| a | "a" | said *a* as in *bad* |
| b | "be" | said *be* as in *bed* |
| c | "ce" | said *tse* as in *eight seven* |
| d | "de" | said *de* as in *den* |
| e | "e" | said *e* as in *den* |
| f | "ef | said *eff* as in *Jeff* |
| g | "gie" | said *gye* as in *dog yes* |
| h | "ha" as in *happy*, but with a raspy Polish **h** (*see p.19*) – you can also call it "samo ha" to distinguish it from **ch** | |
| i | "i" | said *ee* as in *feet* |
| j | "jot" | sounds like *yacht* |
| k | "ka" | said *ca* as in *cat* |
| l | "el" | said *ell* as in *bell* |

| *letter* | *formal "letter name"* | |
|---|---|---|
| m | "em" | said *em* as in *hem* |
| n | "en" | said *en* as in *hen* |
| o | "o" | said *o* as in *dog* |
| p | "pe" | said *pe* as in *pet* |
| r | "er" | sounds like *air*, but with a Polish rolled **r** (*see p.19*) |
| s | "es" | said *ess* as in *mess* |
| t | "te" | said *te* as in *tennis* |
| u | "u" said *oo* as in *too*, also called "**u otwarte**" *open u* to distinguish it from **ó** (which is "**u zamknięte**" *closed u*) | |
| w | "wu" | said *voo* as in *voodoo* |
| y | "igrek" | like the *egrec* in *be Greco-Roman* |
| z | "zet" | like *zed* with a *t* |

*PS The warning from p.15 about the sound descriptions applies here too. Go to www.grijben.com/alphabet/pl to hear the sounds.*

## Formal "letter names" vs informal "letter sounds"

The table (p.30) shows what you could call the formal "letter names" of the main letters of the alphabet (*for accented letters, see p.32*). Use these when you want to spell something out and you'll always be understood.

However, you should know that Polish speakers themselves often use what you could call informal "letter sounds". Now, that's different from English, where it tends to only be children who use letter sounds (for example, "*w*" would be "*vuh*"), while adults tend to use letter names ("*double yoo*"). In Polish, though, it's normal (even for adults) to use the letter sounds – for example, **m** could be said *muh* as in *mug* instead of *em* as in *hem*.

On the other hand, for abbreviations and acronyms, the formal letter names are the norm. For example, **PKP*** is said "*pe ka pe*" not "*puh kuh puh*", and **SMS** is said "*es em es*" not "*suh muh suh*".

***Polskie Koleje Państwowe**
*Polish National Railway*

## Double, capital and lowercase letters

When you're spelling something out, you might also find the following useful:

| **podwójny** | **wielka litera** | **mała litera** |
|---|---|---|
| *double* | *capital letter* | *lowercase letter* |

Note that **wielka** and **mała** just mean *big* and *small*. And like **podwójny**, they're adjectives, so you have to match them to the noun (e.g. masculine, feminine, neuter), for example **wielki ef** *capital f* but **wielka ka** *capital k*. Here's an example of how to use them to spell something:

**Cardiff pisze się wielkie ce, a, er, de, i, podwójne ef.**
*Cardiff is spelled capital c, a, r, d, i, double f.*

For a double letter, particularly in casual language, people also say (using "*ff*" as the example) **ef ef** *ff* or **dwa razy ef** *two times f*.

*For other symbols, such as a hyphen for a double-barrelled name, see Punctuation on p.34.*

## Special letter names

When spelling out a word, the special letters ą ć ę ł ń ó ś ź and ż are slightly tricky, in that you need to get the pronunciation bang on to be sure you'll be understood, given that, for example, ź and ż are similar but distinct sounds to a Polish ear.

If in doubt, you can make it clear by describing the letter in words instead ("*z with a line*" etc, as below).

| *letter* | *formal "letter name"* | | *informal "letter sound" (if different)* | *description in words* |
|---|---|---|---|---|
| ą | "ą" | said *ong* – sort of (*see p.20*) | | ą z ogonkiem<br>*a with a little tail* |
| ć | "cie" | said sort of like the *che* in *check* (*see p.22 for how to say* ć/ci) | said *chu* as in *chuck* or *chee* as in *cheese* | ce z kreską<br>*c with a line* |
| ę | "ę" | said *ew(n)* – sort of (*see p.21*) | | e z ogonkiem<br>*e with a little tail* |
| ł | "eł" | said *eo* like the *airw* in *hair wax* | said *wi* as in *win* | el z kreską ukośną<br>*l with a slanted line* |
| ń | "eń" | said *eny* as in *hen yes* | said *nyu* in *hen yuck* | en z kreską<br>*n with a line* |
| ó | n/a – use the description instead | | → | u zamknięte<br>*a closed oo* (to distinguish it from u) |
| ś | "eś" | said *esh* as in *mesh* – sort of (*see p.22*) | | es z kreską<br>*s with a line* |
| ź | "ziet" (*see p.22 for how to say* zi) | | | zet z kreską<br>*z with a line* |
| ż | "żet" (*see p.22 for how to say* ż) | | | zet z kropką<br>*z with a dot* |

### Names of the lines and dots

Here is a quick summary of the names of the lines and dots that are part of the special Polish letters, using **ć**, **ę**, **ł** and **ż** as examples:

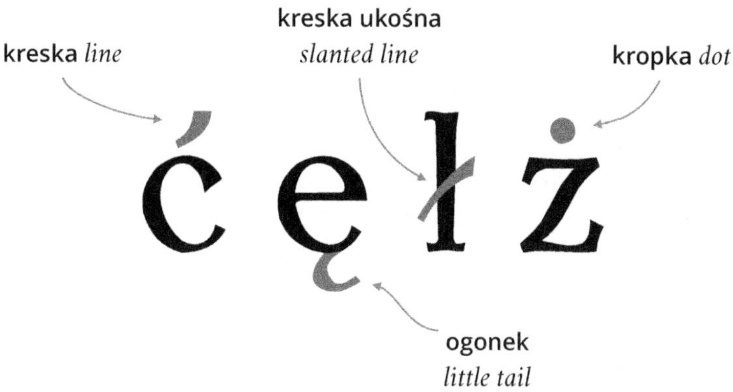


### Alternative names

While you can happily use the "descriptions" given in the table on p.32, don't be surprised if you see these letters described using other aliases. For example, **ó** can be **u zamknięte** as in the table, but it's also sometimes known as **ó zamknięte, o z kreską, ó z kreską, o kreskowane** or **ó kreskowane.** Similarly, **ń** can be known as **ni.** And **ż** can be **samo żet** (to distinguish it from **rz**).

## Names of foreign letters

You may also need to name these letters if you're spelling out foreign (non-Polish) words or abbreviations – or for spelling out your own name, perhaps:

| *letter* | *formal "letter name"* |
|---|---|
| q | "ku" like the *coo* in *coot* |
| v | "fau" like the *fou* in *foul* |
| x | "iks" *eeks* as in *weeks* |

# Punctuation

Here are the names for common punctuation marks, and some special characters (that you might need for, say, Internet purposes).

| | |
|---|---|
| . | **kropka** *dot* |
| , | **przecinek** *comma* |
| ! | **wykrzyknik** *exclamation mark* |
| ? | **znak zapytania** *question mark* |
| / | **ukośnik** *(forward) slash* |
| \ | **ukośnik wsteczny** *backslash* |
| - | **łącznik** *hyphen* |
| – | **myślnik** *dash* |
| : | **dwukropek** *colon* |
| ; | **średnik** *semicolon* |
| ... | **wielokropek** *ellipsis* |
| ' | **apostrof** *apostrophe* |
| * | **gwiazdka** *asterisk* |
| @ | **małpa** *at* |
| # | **kratka** *hash* |
| ^ | **cyrkumfleks** *circumflex* |
| _ | **znak podkreślenia** *underscore* |
| & | **et** *ampersand* |
| ( ) | **nawiasy okrągłe** *round brackets/parentheses* |
| [ ] | **nawiasy kwadratowe** *square brackets* |
| { } | **nawiasy klamrowe** *curly brackets/braces* |
| < > | **nawiasy ostrokątne** *angle brackets/chevrons* |
| „ ” | **cudzysłów** *quotation marks* |
| « » | **cudzysłów niemiecki** *secondary quotation marks* |

The use of punctuation marks in Polish is broadly similar to English. There are a few things you may notice though, as follows.

### Abbreviations

In Polish, an abbreviation ends with a full stop (for example **inżynier** → **inż.** *engineer*), unless it ends with the same letter as the full word it represents (for example **doktor** → **dr** *doctor*).

Note that when many common multi-word phrases are abbreviated, they only get one full stop at the end (for example **i tak dalej** → **itd.** *and so on*).

### Commas

There are different rules on the use of commas in Polish compared to English. For example, a comma is used (warning: technical) to separate a subordinate clause from the rest of a sentence, even before **że** *that*.

**Ona powiedziała, że ser był stary.** *She said that the cheese was old.*

## Apostrophes

When an ending is tagged onto a non-Polish word whose last letter is not pronounced, an apostrophe precedes the ending. For example:

**alfabet Morse'a** *the Morse code*
**jestem ze Steve'em** *I am with Steve*
**pies Harry'ego** *Harry's dog*

NB By convention, the **y** is not pronounced in forms like this.

## Speech marks for dialogue

The most common symbol used to mark dialogue (in novels, for example) is a long dash (to be specific, it's typically an em dash). The dashes separate speech from non-speech.

**— Hura, wygrałem! — krzyknął Bartek.**
**— Gratulacje — odpowiedziała Ewa.**
**— Dziękuję.**
**— Do jutra więc. — Ewa od razu wskoczyła do wody.**

*"Hurrah, I won!" shouted Bartek.*
*"Congratulations," replied Ewa.*
*"Thank you."*
*"See you tomorrow then." Immediately, Ewa jumped into the water.*

Points to note:

- There's a dash at the start of each spoken part.
- There's a dash at the end of speech *only* if it's needed to separate the speech from a non-spoken part (so no dash on the third line above).
- Where you would end speech with a comma in English (the second line above), there is no comma in Polish.
- But where the speech is followed by a standalone sentence (the fourth line above), there is a full stop before the dash.

## Speech marks for quotes

While dashes — are used for dialogue as above, you use quotation marks „ " to mark quoted words, book titles, etc. within a sentence. For example:

**Czy przeczytałaś „Solaris" Stanisława Lema?**
*Have you read "Solaris" by Stanisław Lem?*

For a quote within a quote, you use different quotation marks: « ». As in this example:

**Słyszałem, że „bez wątpienia «Solaris» to jego najlepsza książka".**
*I heard that "without a doubt, 'Solaris' is his best book".*

# Typing Polish characters

Electronic devices change all the time, so the best approach on your equipment may differ, but here's some useful advice on how to type the special Polish characters (ą ć ę ł ń ó ś ż ź).

### Copy and paste from the web

Perhaps the simplest way, and great if all else fails, is to just bring up a web page that has the Polish characters, and copy them from there. Try *www.grijben.com/alphabet/pl*, for example.

### Mac shortcuts

At the time of writing, Apple Mac users can use simple keyboard shortcuts for a lot of foreign accent letters – but not for Polish ones. The only shortcuts are for ó and Ó.

Hold down the Option key then press the E key, let go, and then press the O key for ó (or Shift and O for Ó).

| *letter* | *Mac shortcut* |
|---|---|
| ó | Option + E, O |
| Ó | Option + E, Shift + O |

(That's a bit limited. Keep reading.)

### Put your keyboard in Polish mode

If you can put your keyboard into "Polish mode", it becomes dead easy to type the special letters. For example, on the Windows PC I'm using to type this here book, I just hold the right *Alt* key and tap a letter to give the Polish "accented" character, such as *Alt* + *S* = ś.

The challenge is that the way to set the keyboard language layout depends on your exact operating system (Windows, Mac OS, Linux, etc). I won't attempt to give advice here, as it'll likely be out of date by the time I finish typing this paragraph. Your best bet is to ask the Internet: search for "Polish keyboard layout" and the name of your operating system to see what's possible.

### Touchscreens: tap and hold the letter

Again, this will depend on your particular device, but this is at least worth trying on your phone or other touchscreen keyboard: tap and hold the normal letter to get some special options. For example, tap and hold a and see if ą appears as an option.

## Alt + number pad, HTML codes

Using *Alt* and the number pad is an option if you are using a computer that's running Windows and your keyboard has a number pad (the numbers in a block on the right-hand side). It works in most places in most programs. An advantage is that you don't have to set the keyboard to Polish mode, so it's good if, say, you're using someone else's computer and/or don't want to start digging through the settings.

To type the special character, first make sure the keyboard is in *Num Lock* mode, so the number pad keys are working as numbers, not cursor keys etc. Now, press the *Alt* key and keep holding it down while you type the number shown below on the number pad. When you release the *Alt* key, the character should appear.

The HTML codes are for when you're coding web pages. These are the easy-to-read HTML versions, but you can instead convert the Alt codes into HTML (e.g. ą is ą and ć is ć) if you prefer.

| *letter* | *Alt code* | *HTML* | *letter* | *Alt code* | *HTML* |
|---|---|---|---|---|---|
| ą | 0261 | &aogon | ś | 0347 | ś |
| Ą | 0260 | Ą | Ś | 0346 | Ś |
| ć | 0263 | ć | ź | 0378 | ź |
| Ć | 0262 | Ć | Ź | 0377 | Ź |
| ę | 0281 | ę | ż | 0380 | ż |
| Ę | 0280 | Ę | Ż | 0379 | Ż |
| ł | 0322 | ł | „ | 0132 | „ |
| Ł | 0321 | Ł | ” | 0148 | ” |
| ń | 0324 | ń | « | 0171 | « |
| Ń | 0323 | Ń | » | 0187 | » |
| ó | 0243 | ó | — | 0151 | &#emdash |
| Ó | 0211 | Ó | | | |

# Handwriting quirks

It's worth being aware of the common Polish handwriting quirks so you don't get thrown when deciphering shop signs/love notes/ parking tickets/etc. Here's a traditional handwritten (cursive) Polish alphabet, and some highlighted oddities (i.e. differences from printed forms) you may come across in people's handwriting.

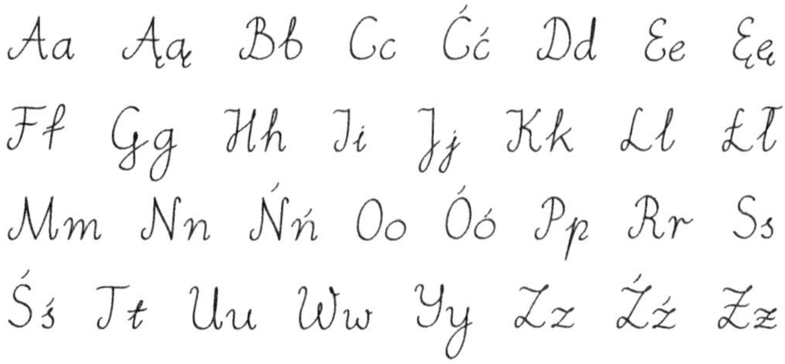

yes, this is a rounded capital **E**, not a backwards 3

check out the closed loop on the lower case **f**

even a capital **G** can have a loopy descender

the round part of a lower case **p** is sometimes left open

a printed lowercase **ł** has a line in the middle, but in handwriting it's at the top – use this trick in your own writing to help mark out your **ł** from your **t**

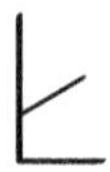

sometimes you see an **Ł** like this on handwritten signs, where the stroke doesn't cross the upright

sneakily, the top bar and tail on this **I** (top) makes it similar to a printed **J** – but the actual written **J** (bottom) gets a funky closed-loop descender

these are just an alternative way to write **Ż** and **ż**

# Putting it all together

The beauty of the Polish writing system is that although there are rules and exceptions to learn, once you know them, you can tackle pretty much any word you come across. (That's completely unlike English, where the connection between letters and sounds is often pretty loose.) Here are some examples of how you can use the rules from this book to sound out some Polish words.

**rz** stands for a single sound similar to the *s* in *treasure*, as described on p.16 and p.23

the r is rolled, as mentioned on p.19

## przepraszam

some combinations of sounds can be tricky, especially if you don't get them in English, but p.13 has notes on how to practise

the stress is on the last-but-one syllable, as covered on p.27

**sz** stands for a single sound similar to the *sh* in *shark*, as described on p.22

generally, an **a** is like the *a* in *hat* wherever it appears, as in **Panama** on p.12

## wiewiórka

**w** stands for a sound like the *v* in *very*, as on p.15

the **i** "softens" a preceding **w** – in effect, instead of the full *ea* as in *pea* sound for the **i**, it's more like the *y* in *yes*, as on p.17

**ć** is similar to the *ch* in *cheese*, as on p.23

## europeizować

**eu** is said as though it were **eł**, while the **e** and **i** are said separately (not slid together), as on p.26

**z** is said like the *z* in *zoo*, as on p.15

# Quiz

Check your knowledge by answering these questions.
The topics covered are in the same order as they appear in the book.

*For answers, see p. 46.*

1. How many letters are there in the Polish alphabet?
2. List all eight Polish vowels.
3. Put these words into dictionary order:
   **dołu dębowy dać dół dach**
   **dwa dąb dolny decyzja dawny**
4. Which Polish letter has a sound like the *ts* in *gnats* or *satsuma*?
5. Which Polish letter sounds like the *w* in *week* or *runway*?
6. True or false? The Polish letter **ń** sounds like the *nn* in *funny*.
7. Which two Polish vowels have the same sound as the *oo* in *moo*?
8. Which single Polish letter has the same sound as **rz**?
9. For each of these words, say whether the **p** is a "hard" consonant or is "softened" by the **i**.
   **pić małpi piec piłka piżama karpi**
   **pierogi lipiec czasopismo kupić piątek**
   **podpis szpital sklepi sypialnia**
10. What is the difference in the pronunciation of **rany** and **ranny**?
11. True or false? In Polish, **ch** and **h** have the same sound.
12. In colloquial pronunciation, what sound does **ą** typically make in these words?
    **trójkąt gołąb ręką wąski wziął**
    **kąpiel mąka są mądry pociąg mąż**
13. In colloquial pronunciation, what sound does **ę** typically make in these words?
    **zęby piętro idę pędzel dostępne wzięła ręką**

14. Which of these letter combinations is the odd one out?
    **dź  dż  drz**

15. What is the difference in sound between **mieć** and **miecz**?

16. The following are all voiced consonants. For each voiced consonant, what would be the nearest unvoiced equivalent?
    **d  g  z  ż  b  w  ź**

17. In Polish, letters such as **k**, **p** and **t** are "unaspirated". What does unaspirated mean?

18. What is the sound of the underlined vowels in these words?
    **zaimek  stoi  auto  euforia  hiena  ciemny  siano**

19. Which syllable is stressed in each of these words?
    **Auto  ciasto  impreza  lodowisko  podwieczorek**
    **ananas  ananasowy  trzysta  czterysta**
    **siedemset  matematyka  prezydent  Ameryka**

20. Sing (or write) the whole English alphabet, but using the Polish formal letter names.

21. Give the formal letter names, and descriptions in words, of these Polish letters:
    **ą  ć  ę  ł  ń  ó  ś  ź  ż**

22. Give the Polish names for these punctuation marks:
    **.  ,  !  ?  *  @  /  :**

23. Give the English names for these punctuation marks:
    **łącznik  myślnik  kratka  znak podkreślenia**
    **średnik  apostrof  nawiasy zwykłe**

24. Which abbreviations below should end with a full stop?
    **doktor → dr  inżynier → inż  i tym podobne → itp**
    **godzina → godz  licencjat → lic  magister → mgr**

25. A Polish speaker has written down some English words using Polish spelling. What were the English words?
    **łał  fysz  bajsykl  fasynejt  dżinz  fridż  junik**

# Index

# Hear the sounds from this book

All of the sounds covered in this book
are freely available to listen to online.

Go to *www.grijben.com/alphabet/pl*
to find the videos and hear the sounds.

## Illustrations



## Answers to Quiz questions on p.40–41

1. 32
2. a, ą, e, ę, i, o, ó, y
3. dach, dać, dawny, dąb, decyzja, dębowy, dolny, dołu, dół, dwa
4. c
5. ł
6. False. It sounds like the *ny* in *canyon*.
7. ó and u
8. ż
9. pić hard, głupi hard, piec soft, piłka hard, piżama hard, karpi hard, pierogi soft, lipiec soft, czasopismo hard, kupić hard, piątek soft, podpis hard, szpital hard, sklepi hard, sypialnia soft
10. In ranny, the double n is either sounded as a single, extended n, or as two separate letters.
11. True
12. *See p.20*
13. *See p.21*
14. dź (dż and drz have the same sound)
15. The ć in mieć is said with the Y position; the cz in miecz is said with the R position (*see p.20–21*)
16. t, k, s, sz, p, f, ś
17. They are said without a puff of air.
18. a, be, ce, de, e, ef, gie, ha, i, jot, ka, el, em, en, o, pe, ku, er, es, te, u (otwarte), fau, wu, iks, igrek, zet
19. a z ogonkiem, c z kreską, e z ogonkiem, l z kreską ukośną, n z kreską, u zamknięte, s z kreską, z z kreską, z z kropką
20. auto, ciasto, impreza, lodowisko, podwieczorek, ananas, ananasowy, trzysta, czterysta, siedemset, matematyka, prezydent, Ameryka
21. kropka, przecinek, wykrzyknik, znak zapytania, gwiazdka, małpa, ukośnik
22. hyphen, dash, hash, underscore, semicolon, apostrophe, round brackets/parentheses
23. inż., itp., godz., lic.
24. wow, fish, bicycle, fascinate, jeans/genes, fridge, unique

# Also available from Grijben

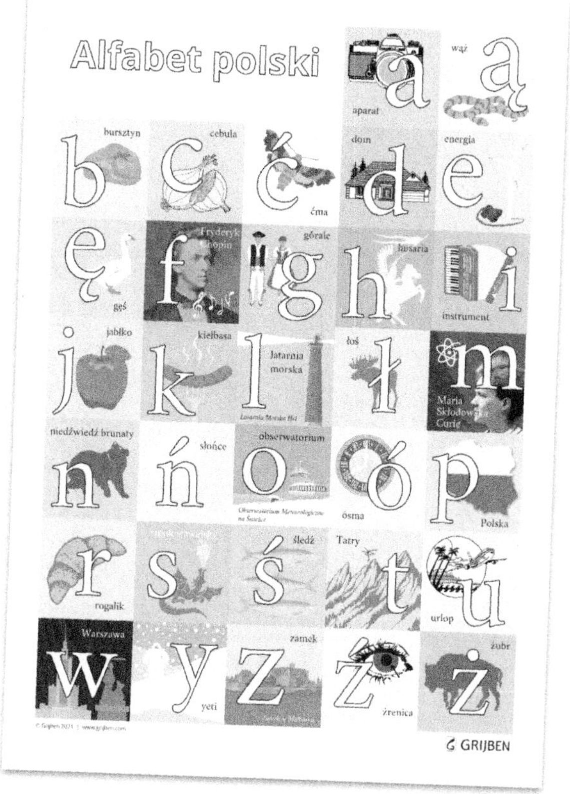


A full-colour poster featuring all 32 letters of the Polish alphabet, from a to ż.

Available in a range of sizes.

The illustrations include Polish landmarks and historical figures, including Nobel-prize winner Marie Skłodowska Curie and the famous Malbork Castle.

Visit *www.grijben.com/books-etc/posters* for more details.

★★★★★

*"Lovely print. Great quality, colors, and word/topic illustrations for each letter." Etsy customer review*

Printed in Great Britain
by Amazon

27467978R00030